THE INDIAN LITERATURE

A STUDY OF THE CLASSIC INDIAN POETRY, PROSE, AND LITERATURE

DR. JAGADEESH PILLAI

Made with ❤ on the Notion Press Platform
www.notionpress.com

|| "Dedicated to all who seek to understand and appreciate Indian culture and tradition." ||

Contents

Contents

Prayer

"Om Sham No Mitra Sham Varunah Sham No Bhavatvaryamaa,Sham Na Indro Brihaspatih Sham No Vishnururukramah,Namo Brahmane Namaste Vaayo Tvameva Pratyaksham, Brahmaasi Tvaameva Pratyaksham Brahma Vadishyaami,Rtam Vadishyaami Satyam Vadishyaami,Tanmaamavatu Tadvaktaaramavatu Avatu Maam Avatu Vaktaaram,Om Shantih Shantih Shantih"

This mantra implies: Om. May Mitra bestow us with blessings, may Varuna grant us favor, may Aryama show us kindness, may Indra grant us prosperity, may Brihaspati bestow us with wisdom, and may Vishnu, who has vast coverage, grant us with his benevolence. We salute Lord Brahma and Lord Vayu, the embodiment of Brahman. We speak with integrity and truth, may it protect us and our teacher.
Om, peace, peace, and peace.

About The Author

Dr. Jagadeesh Pillai is a renowned Guinness World Record holder, writer, and researcher hailing from Varanasi, also known as the abode of Lord Shiva. With a Ph.D. in Vedic Science and a range of creative ideas and achievements, he is a true polymath. He is the author of more than 100 books including Research Publications. Although his roots can be traced back to Kerala, the people of Varanasi hold him in high regard and affectionately consider him one of their own.

Dr. Pillai has achieved four Guinness World Records in the following subjects:

"Script to Screen" - In this record, Dr. Pillai produced and directed an animation film within the shortest time possible, breaking the previous record set by Canadians. He has also received numerous national and international awards and recognitions for this achievement.

Longest Line of Postcards - For this record, Dr. Pillai created a line of 16,300 postcards on the occasion of the 163rd anniversary of Indian Postal Day. The event also included a questionnaire about the Indian flag.

Largest Poster Awareness Campaign - Dr. Pillai designed an awareness campaign on the subject of "Beti Bachao - Beti Padhao" (Save the Girl Child - Educate the Girl Child) to achieve this record.

Largest Envelope - In tribute to the Indian Prime Minister's

"Make in India" initiative, Dr. Pillai created a 4000 square meter envelope using waste paper to achieve this record.

Attempted - **70000 Candles on a 210 kg Cake** - To celebrate the 70th Indian Independence Day, Dr. Pillai attempted to light 70,000 candles on a 210 kg cake, which was recorded in World Records India.

Attempted - **Documentary on Dhamek Stupa of Sarnath in 17 Languages** - Dr. Pillai attempted to create a documentary on the Dhamek Stupa of Sarnath, dubbing it in 17 different languages. The result of this attempt is currently awaiting confirmation from the Guinness World Records.

Dr. Pillai is skilled in teaching the Bhagavad Gita, a Hindu scripture, and is popular among young people. He has helped many young people improve their lives through his motivational teachings.

In addition to teaching, he has composed and sung numerous Sanskrit Bhajans and patriotic songs.

He has also written and directed several short films and documentaries for awareness campaigns, and has volunteered with the police in both UP and Kerala to spread awareness about various issues through videos and photography.

Incredibly, he has produced and directed over 100 documentaries about the city of Varanasi, all on his own.

He has also helped and guided more than 25 boys and girls to achieve world records through creative and innovative methods. He is a multifaceted person who uses his intellect and the blessings given to him by God to excel in various areas. He is both a teacher and a student, always learning and teaching, and is able to master any subject he comes across.

He is a selfless social activist and motivational speaker who has overcome struggles and failures to become a successful and enthusiastic individual with a rich life experience.

In addition to his work with the Bhagavad Gita, he is also an efficient Tarot card reader, Astro-Vastu consultant, and a talented singer and composer. He has sung the entire Ram Charita Manas and Bhagavad Gita in his own compositions, and has sung the phrase "Lokah Samastha Sukhino Bhavantu" in 50 different languages. He is currently working on a detailed and scientific study of Vedas, Upanishads, Puranas, and the Bhagavad Gita. He has also composed and sung the Hanuman Chalisa and Gayatri Mantra in 108 and 1008 different compositions, respectively.

Awards - Four Times Guinness World Records, Winner of Mahatma Gandhi Vishwa Shanti Puraskar, Mahatma Gandhi Global Peace Ambassador, Kashi Ratna Award, Dr. APJ Abdul Kalam Motivational Person of the Year 2017, Mother Teresa Award, Indira Gandhi Priyadarshini Award, Bharat Vikas Ratna Award, Udyog Ratna Award, Vigyan Prasar Award, Poorvanchal Ratn Samman.

Preface

Indian Literature is a vast and rich tapestry of stories, poetry and intellectual thought. It is one of the oldest recorded literature in the world, dating back to the beginnings of written language in the Indus Valley Civilization. This literature has evolved over many centuries and its various genres, storytelling traditions, languages, authors and styles span a wide range of India's history and culture.

Classic Indian Poetry is one of the core genres in Indian Literature. Traditional Indian Poetry utilizes techniques and themes taken from classical Sanskrit and Tamil literary forms, often featuring rich images, metaphors, and abstract concepts. The Mahabharata, one of the most noteworthy pieces of Indian literature, is comprised mainly of poetic ballads expressing the ancient Indian epics and is regarded as one the largest epics ever written. Other famous pieces of classic Indian Poetry include the Bhagavad Gita, Ramayana and the works of poet-saints like Kabirdas and Tulsidas.

Classic Indian prose is another important genre of Indian literature. The works of Kalidasa and Banabhatta are renowned for their poetic elegance and literary mastery. In the field of fiction, the works of Vikram Seth and R. K. Narayan have attained iconic status both in India and abroad. Their stories celebrated India's cultural heritage, highlighting various themes such as caste and gender, while offering a fresh perspective to Indian literature.

Indian literature has also produced several works of non-fiction, including historical chronicles and religious texts. The Vedic period is known for its valuable discoveries of ancient texts such as the Upanishads and the Rigveda. Authors like Swami Vivekananda, Swami Dayananda Saraswati, Nelson Mandela and Mahatma Gandhi have written such masterpieces that have been cherished by generations.

Indian Literature remains alive and relevant in the 21st century, this is evident in the works of current authors like Amitav Ghosh and Arundhati Roy. These authors have enriched the literary heritage of India with vivid stories, informed conversations and thought provoking perspectives.

Ultimately, Indian Literature is an awe-inspiring proposition with its centuries-old continuities and numerous evolutions. The diverse forms of texts, the plethora of writers, along with the common threads of storytelling, poetry, and historical and social discourse combine to create a living and pulsating form of literature.

The Indian literature is a rich and diverse body of work that spans thousands of years. From the ancient Vedic texts to the modern literature of today, Indian literature has always been an integral part of the Indian culture and society. This book, "The Indian Literature: A Study Of The Classic Indian Poetry, Prose, And Literature" is an attempt to explore and understand the classic Indian literature in all its forms. Through this book, we will delve into the history, themes, and styles of the Indian literature and examine the works of some of the most renowned Indian authors and poets. This book is aimed at both scholars and general readers who are interested in understanding the Indian literature and its significance in the Indian cultural and literary landscape.

ONE

An Overview of Indian Literature: From Ancient to Modern Times

Indian literature is a rich and diverse field, with a long and complex history that spans thousands of years. From the earliest Vedic and epic poems to contemporary postcolonial literature, Indian literature has evolved and transformed in response to the social, cultural, and political contexts of the time.

The earliest examples of Indian literature can be found in the Vedas, the oldest sacred texts of Hinduism. These texts, which date back to around 1500 BCE, include hymns, prayers, and rituals that were passed down orally for centuries before being written down. The Vedas are considered to be the foundation of Indian literature and culture, and their influence can be seen in later Indian literature, including the epic poems such as the Ramayana and the Mahabharata.

The epic poems, which were written down in Sanskrit between the 4th and 2nd centuries BCE, are considered to be some of the greatest works of Indian literature. They tell the stories of gods and heroes, and offer moral and philosophical teachings. The Bhagavad Gita, a section of the Mahabharata, is a revered Indian scripture, and is considered to be one of the greatest works of Indian literature. It is an epic poem that has been widely studied and discussed for its philosophical and spiritual teachings.

Classical Indian literature, which developed between the 4th and 12th centuries CE, is characterized by its use of the Sanskrit language and its focus on religious and philosophical themes. During this period, Indian literature also began to be written in regional languages like Prakrit and Pali. Prose works such as the Panchatantra and Jataka tales, which are collections of animal fables and moral stories, also emerged during this time.

Medieval Indian literature, which developed between the 12th and 18th centuries CE, is characterized by its religious and spiritual themes. The Sufi and Bhakti movements, which emphasized devotion to God, had a strong influence on Indian literature during this period. The Mughal court also played an important role in promoting literature and the arts, resulting in a rich tradition of poetry and prose in Persian and Urdu.

In the 19th century CE, with the arrival of British colonialism, Indian literature was heavily influenced by Western literary styles and themes. Indian writers began to write in English, and there was a renewed interest in Indian history and culture. This period saw the emergence of the Indian novel and the Indian short story.

Contemporary Indian literature is diverse and varied, reflecting the many different cultures and languages of India. It has been shaped by the experiences of independence, partition, and the ongoing process of nation-building. Indian literature in English, Hindi, Bengali, and other languages has gained recognition around the world.

Indian literature is a rich and diverse field that has evolved and transformed throughout history in response to the social, cultural, and political contexts of the time. From the earliest Vedic and epic poems to contemporary postcolonial literature, Indian literature offers a window into the lives and experiences of the people of India, and has been a source of inspiration, guidance, and entertainment for generations.

"A library is the foundation of a nation."

- Jawaharlal Nehru

This quote by India's first Prime Minister expresses the importance of literature and books as the cornerstone of a great nation.

TWO

Classical Indian Poetry: An Analysis of the Vedic and Epic Poems

Classical Indian poetry has served as an important source of cultural information, literature and art over the centuries. Indian poetry can be divided into two main genres: Vedic and Epic poetry. The Vedic tradition of poetry can be traced all the way back to the Vedic period, approximately 1500-1200 BC. This is a period in which Indian culture was heavily influenced by the religious beliefs of Hinduism and other religions of the ancient subcontinent. Vedic poetry has a significant focus on the divine, moral philosophy and the setting of religious hymns. The Epic tradition of poetry dates from around the same period, but is distinctly different in style and content from the Vedic style. Epic poetry is characterized by vivid, elaborate and highly stylized historical or mythic narratives.

Vedic poetry is composed of four distinct types of verse: riks, sama, yatu and atharvans. A rik is the most basic type of poem in the Vedic tradition and was traditionally used to address gods and goddesses through the invocation of certain desires or prayers. Sama poetry is another type of poem used in Vedic scriptures and is based on rhythmic chanting and dance. Yatu poetry is more closely associated with magic and sorcery and was traditionally used to invoke spiritual powers. Finally, atharvans are used in rituals when asking for blessings or protection.

In contrast to the Vedic tradition of poetry, Epic poetry has a distinctly different style and content. Epic poems, such as the Indian Epics, are typically written in a grandiose style and focus on larger-than-life themes such as heroism, courage, and honor. Epic poems often serve as a source of cultural guidance and values, as they tell stories of the gods, goddesses, and important figures that are often held in high regard by Indian cultures. Additionally, Epic poems are often full of metaphors and symbols which often provide insight into the ethical and moral way of life of the ancient Indian peoples.

Classical Indian poetry is an important source of literature, cultural information and art in India. The two main genres of Indian poetry, Vedic and Epic, have many distinct differences but are both essential for understanding the ancient cultures of India. Vedic poetry is characterized by religious invocations and magical chants, while Epic poems have grandiose stylistic elements with heavy focus on moral and heroic themes. Together, Vedic and Epic poetry form the foundation of Indian literature, culture, and art and provide insight into the values and beliefs of the ancient peoples of India.

"A nation's literature is its foundation."
- Mahatma Gandhi

Gandhi suggests that literature is essential to the culture and identity of a nation, reflecting its values and worldview.

THREE

The Bhagavad Gita: A Study of Its Literary and Philosophical Significance

The Bhagavad Gita is an ancient Hindu scripture that is deep in philosophical and literary significance. It contains teachings of Krishna to the prince Arjuna and gives insight into the struggles faced in this human form. It is believed to have been written in 1000 BCE, making it one of the oldest scriptures still in existence.

From a literary point of view, the Bhagavad Gita is a complex and nuanced collection of poetic dialogues between Krishna and Arjuna. It presents us with a plot involving two sets of characters in a battlefield, in which

Arjuna's doubts and inner struggles are voiced. The narrative structure of the Gita as well is renowned for its elegant composition and vivid descriptions of the battlefields and its characters.

From a philosophical perspective, the Bhagavad Gita is an important scripture that provides advice to those facing indecision in life. It discusses fundamental human philosophy such as Dharma, Karma, and the meaning of life. It is also famous for presenting the three paths on which humans can progress towards self-realization, known as Jnana Yoga, Bhakti Yoga and Karma Yoga. With its deep understanding of the human mind and emphasis on divinity and unity, the wisdom of the Gita can be applied to practically any situation, making it a timeless text.

The Bhagavad Gita is also noteworthy for its incorporation of both duality and non-duality. It speaks of the duality of Nature, the existence of the physical world and the spiritual world, while at the same time emphasizing the unity of all souls and the need to find inner peace and contentment. Its message to seek the highest truth and inner silence transcends social, religious and regional boundaries and resounds universally.

The Bhagavad Gita is an ancient collection of scriptures with immense literary and philosophical significance. Its insights into the mysteries of life and its timeless spiritual wisdom captivates both modern and ancient readers alike. Its wisdom has withstood the test of time, and true to its teachings, the Gita continues to inspire self-realization and lasting peace.

"Happiness resides not in possessions and not in gold, the feeling of happiness dwells in the soul."
- Rabindranath Tagore

This quote reminds us that happiness comes from within and doesn't depend on our material possessions or money.

FOUR

Classical Indian Prose: An Analysis of the Panchatantra and Jataka Tales

Classical Indian Prose refers to ancient and traditional works of literature written in the languages of India. It spans many centuries, from the Vedic period of the 2nd millennium BCE to the early 19th century CE. This literature had a profound impact on the culture and literature of South Asia and beyond, offering a rich source of myths, stories, poems and teachings. Two of the most iconic examples of Classical Indian Prose are the Panchatantra and the Jataka Tales.

The Panchatantra is an ancient Sanskrit collection of stories compiled around 200 BCE by Indian scholar Vishnu Sharma. It consists of five books of moral stories and is a classic of world literature. It is believed to have been written for the purpose of educating the sons of a powerful king and the stories feature animals, plants and birds as characters. The Panchatantra is renowned for its moral content, using wit and humor to deliver profound messages about life, death, freedom and responsibility. The stories depict animals who possess human qualities and teach important lessons.

The Jataka Tales are a collection of nearly 600 stories and fables attributed to the Buddha and compiled dating back as far as 300 BCE. These tales are rich with lessons of morality and practicality, featuring human and animal characters who exemplify noble to despicable values. They are considered to be some of the finest and most popular stories of the Indian tradition. The images and characters in the stories teach Buddhist virtues such as morality, patience and compassion.

Both the Panchatantra and the Jataka Tales are remarkable examples of classical Indian prose which have stood the test of time. They are full of wisdom and wit, using memorable stories to teach timeless lessons about life and death, freedom and responsibility. The stories of these two collections have influenced generations of writers and readers and continue to inspire us today.

"Love does not cope well with doubt."
- Nirad C. Chaudhuri

Love needs to be sure, free from any fear or hesitation, in order to grow and be strong.

♡♡♡

FIVE

Medieval Indian Literature: An Exploration of Sufi and Bhakti Poetry

Medieval Indian literature has long been one of the great treasures of world literature. It is renowned for its rich variety of styles and genres, such as Sufi and Bhakti poetry. Sufi and Bhakti poetry offer insight into the religious and spiritual practices of medieval India, and are some of the most enduring and influential features of Indian literature.

Sufi poetry is rooted in Islamic traditions, often presenting themes of divine love and devotion. Sufi poets such as

Khwaja Moinuddin Chishti, Rumi and Amir Khusrau used language and powerful imagery to explore the relationship between a worshiper and the divine. Central to their works was the concept of a journey or purification, with the ultimate goal of achieving a spiritual union with God. This union was symbolized by the metaphor of a bride and her lover. In his poem "The Love that is Both Divine and Human," renowned Sufi poet Rumi wrote, "Lover and Beloved, how can I describe their union? Water and waves, how can I show their relation?"

In contrast to Sufi poetry, Bhakti poetry celebrates devotion to Hindu gods and goddesses. The Bhakti movement, which originated in the 7th century, was a popular expression of Hinduism with heavy focus on love and devotion to deities. Poets such as Mirabai, Kabir and Tukaram wrote works stressing the importance of personally loving one's chosen god and goddess, often in the form of an intimate relationship. Rich imagery was key to these poems, with poets often describing their body as the temple and their beloved deity as the god residing within. Mirabai wrote, "The Lord is my beloved, nothing else I desire. Like a wave and water, my body and soul both move to Him."

Together, Sufi and Bhakti poetry have been immensely influential in shaping medieval Indian literature. With their vivid imagery and powerful metaphors, these poets explore the complex relationship between worshiper and divine. They offer insight into the unique spirituality of medieval India and remain some of the most captivating works of Indian literature.

"No nation is great without its books."
- Harivansh Rai Bachchan

Books are the vehicles of knowledge, values and wisdom. A nation's greatness lies in its books.

SIX

THE MUGHAL COURT AND ITS LITERARY CONTRIBUTIONS

The Mughal court was the center of imperial political power, and it also had significant social and cultural influence over the lands that it ruled. This was especially the case in terms of literature, as the court acted as a sort of cultural center of production and consumption. Imperial patronage of literature, especially poetry and prose, had an enormous impact on the literary growth that took place during the Mughal period.

Beginning in the sixteenth and seventeenth centuries, court poets grew in influence. The poetic style of the time became richer and more sophisticated due to the patronage of Mughal rulers, particularly Emperor Akbar. He was especially known for his taste in literature and the arts and worked to foster a "progressive" attitude towards knowledge, literature, and the sciences. Poets typically worked within the divan format and followed the conventions found in their predecessors, such as forms of Persian ghazals, quatrains, and mystic poetry. At the court of Babur, for example, poetry was particularly popular and well-respected as an art form.

The wide range of poetic styles that were created served to advance Mughal court literature overall. This was especially the case with Persian literature, which was heavily associated with the court. Akbar particularly sought to advance Persian literature within his court and encourages Mughal writers to explore new literary forms, such as the masnavi and Persian prose. The Mughal court was also responsible for the development of the Urdu language and its literature. This was due to its mixing of Persian and Hindi into a new language, as well as its patronage of Urdu authors and its support of Urdu poets.

The output of Mughal court literature greatly increased during the 1700s, particularly with the advent of the govt. of Shah Jahan. He was particularly famous for his patronage of the arts and is known for sponsoring the construction of the Taj Mahal. He was also responsible for the commission of many beautiful manuscripts, such as the Padshanamah. Along with the ruler's patronage, other members of the court were also involved in creating literature. For example, the Emperor's daughter, Jahanara, wrote many works of poetry, prose, and philosophy.

The Mughal court had a significant impact on the development of literature. The court's patronage of poetry and prose, as well as its encouragement of new literary forms, created a dynamic and rich literary culture. The output of Mughal court literature included works in Persian, Urdu, and Hindustani, and these works were created by members of the court, such as the Emperor and his daughter. This literary output added to the prestige and sophistication of the court and greatly advanced the literary culture of the Mughal Empire.

"A poem is a gift of emotion."
- Kamala Das

Poetry is a special gift that can evoke deep emotions in the readers.

♡♡♡

SEVEN

Colonialism and Indian Literature: The Impact of British Rule

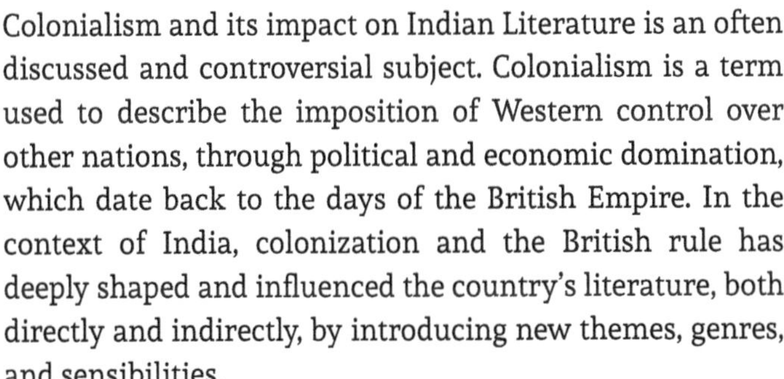

Colonialism and its impact on Indian Literature is an often discussed and controversial subject. Colonialism is a term used to describe the imposition of Western control over other nations, through political and economic domination, which date back to the days of the British Empire. In the context of India, colonization and the British rule has deeply shaped and influenced the country's literature, both directly and indirectly, by introducing new themes, genres, and sensibilities.

During the British colonization in India, a large number

of British writers, including Rudyard Kipling, Robert Clive, and Warren Hastings have created works that portray an Indian culture and lifestyle from an outsider's perspective. At the same time, Indian writers such as Srinivasa Ramanujan, Mulk Raj Anand, and R.K. Narayan have all expressed the effects of colonialism on Indian culture and society in their writings. Kipling's works have provided an insight into the Indian psyche and its classic heritage while Anand's passion for Indian identity and nationhood, coupled with Narayan's strong sense of community and vibrant descriptions of small-town, rural India has all contributed to the Indian literary canon.

On a more fundamental level, the colonization of India and its impact upon literature has had a significant impact upon the development and transformation of the Indian language. Prior to British colonization, English was not widely used and circulated in India, an uncertainty which has been addressed through the introduction of English in schools across India. As a result of the increased availability of English-language education and resources, many Indian writers have begun to incorporate and utilize English into their works to a much greater extent.

In some cases, Indian authors have used English to their advantage by introducing twists and turns to their narratives through the use of grammar and syntax that is both novel and distinct. In addition, Indian authors have shown the ability for English to be effective in expressing the subtleties of human emotions such as sadness, joy, confusion, and frustration.

Overall, British colonization of India and its influence on

Indian literature has had an indelible influence and effect. By introducing themes, genres, and sensibilities, and encouraging the use of the English language, Indian authors have now gained a greater sense of expression and voice, ultimately giving recognition to a nation's unique perspective. These new perspectives have increased appreciation for the literature of India, both in India and abroad, and have powerfully impacted culture and identity in the process.

"Real intangibles of life will be kept alive if only we keep alive books which encapsulate that experience"
-Narendra Modi

This quote is a reminder of the importance of books, which contain the knowledge of the past and can help us appreciate the intangibles of life.

ᑭᑭᑭ

EIGHT

Modern Indian Literature: An Exploration of the Indian Novel

In recent years, Indian literature has seen a rapid growth in terms of both quality and quantity. Among the most notable contributions is the emergence of the modern Indian novel, which has expanded significantly in its range and depth since the dawn of Independence. The Indian novel has served to chronicle the social, political, and cultural changes that have taken place in the postcolonial era and has further explored the implications of traditional literature in modern Indian society.

The modern Indian novel has explored topics such as

poverty, caste discrimination, gender roles, tradition, and urbanization, while also highlighting the various personal struggles of individuals in modern India. These novels have depicted both the positive and negative aspects of life in contemporary India and have provided readers with a diverse array of storylines and characters to relate to.

A key feature of the modern Indian novel is its exploration of the various cultures and linguistic identities of India. Through the depiction of characters and settings, these novels have portrayed the multiple religious, ethnic, and linguistic divisions that compose the Indian nation. Furthermore, the novel has used its stories to encourage a dialogue surrounding the tension created by the increasingly diverse cultures of India.

Perhaps the greatest strength of the modern Indian novel is its clever usage of symbolism and metaphors. These stories often explore complex moral issues by drawing comparisons between objects or situations from the real world and their symbolic counterparts. By making use of these elements, the novel helps readers to comprehend the themes and ideas of the story in a more simplified and effective manner.

Overall, the modern Indian novel has presented an unprecedented insight into society and its associated issues. It has helped to rally empathy and understanding by providing realistic representations of everyday life and the issues its citizens face. Moreover, its usage of symbolism and metaphors has empowered readers to gain a deeper understanding of the stories being told and the ideas being conveyed. It is thus no wonder that the novel has been such a cornerstone of the Indian literary tradition.

"Writing a book is a difficult journey but a fulfilling one."
- Vikram Seth

Books are the fruits of a journey that take the author on a journey towards self-discovery.

ღღღ

NINE

Contemporary Indian Literature: An Exploration of Postcolonial Literature

Postcolonial literature is a type of writing from countries which have experienced colonization by an external power. Contemporary Indian literature is a form of postcolonial literature, arising from centuries of oppression and exploitation under the rule of multinational powers, such as the British Empire. Through an analysis of themes, characters and techniques employed in Indian literature, this essay will explore how Indian literature has evolved to address the continued legacy of colonialism.

A common theme in contemporary Indian literature is a critique of the legacy of colonialism. Authors like Arundhati Roy, Amitav Ghosh, and Salman Rushdie often write about the experience of oppression and subjugation under the rule of the British. Their works often deconstruct colonial powers, expressing the sense of outrage and betrayal felt by the Indian people towards their former oppressor. Moreover, they challenge the idea of colonial superiority by focusing on the resilience, ingenuity and self-sufficiency of Indian culture.

In addition to its critique of colonialism, Indian literature often examines the ways in which the people of India have attempted to cope with their postcolonial identity. Post-colonial critique often takes the form of novels which explore the complex identity crisis often faced by Indians living in a multicultural, post-colonial society. A recurring theme in these works is the idea of navigating between the traditional values of Indian life and the modern, cosmopolitan culture of the West. Through their works, authors like Bapsi Sidhwa explore the conflicting loyalties, feelings of alienation and frustration experienced by those of Indian descent.

Finally, contemporary Indian literature also employs a variety of narrative techniques in order to explore the postcolonial condition. Common elements include the use of flashbacks and dream sequences, which can be used to emphasize subtle emotions and experiences of colonialism. Stream-of-consciousness techniques can also be used effectively to convey the diversity and complexity of Indian life. Furthermore, elements of magical realism are often used to contrast the traditionally idealized image of India with the reality of its post-colonial experience.

Thus, it is clear that contemporary Indian literature has emerged as a powerful form of postcolonial writing. Through its critique of colonialism, exploration of identity and effective use of narrative techniques, Indian authors are able to portray the experience and legacy of colonialism in a unique and powerful way.

"My books forgive me all my faults and guide me to knowledge, which I could never attain with all my study."
- Guru Nanak

This quote reminds us that books can be our greatest teachers, offering knowledge and insight, even when we think we know it all.

ÞÞÞ

TEN

Indian Folk Literature: An Analysis of Oral Traditions

Indian folk literature has been an integral part of the nation's culture for centuries, and its roots can be traced back to the Vedas. From these ancient scriptures emerged a variety of oral traditions, such as epics, myths, legends, ballads, and folk tales, amongst others. Indian folk literature holds an important place in Indian cultural heritage, and it continues to be cherished and studied even today.

Indian folk literature is mainly oral in nature, and as a result, it often contains linguistic qualities and stylistic modes that distinguish it from written literature. Moreover, the themes depicted in Indian folk literature are usually associated with artha, or worldly values. Vibrant storytelling styles, creative stock characters, and the employment of rhyme, meter and other rhythmic devices are all common in Indian folk literature and help to enliven its stories for audiences.

The main purpose of Indian folk literature is to entertain its audience and to educate them on certain values and virtues. Its tales usually revolve around the interplay between various forces, such as good and evil, or grand themes like destiny and justice. Indian folk literature often illustrates exemplary models of individuals and their struggles and triumphs, depicting their moral strength and resilience in the face of adversity. These ideals are then passed on through generations, reinforcing traditional values of community and cooperation.

The stories that make up Indian folk literature have been crafted over centuries, and its oral traditions have been passed down through generations. Its stories reflect the core beliefs held by Indian society, and the vibrant characters and settings employed in them imbue these themes with dynamism and life. This interweaving of entertainment and education is a key feature of Indian folk literature, and it makes it a distinct and powerful form of expression in Indian culture.

In short, Indian folk literature is an important part of the nation's cultural heritage and is steeped in its traditional values and beliefs. Through its narration of tales of moral fortitude and strength, as well as its employment of captivating storytelling techniques, Indian folk literature continues to remain a vibrant, dynamic and timeless form of expression.

❧❧❧

"It is more important to feel the words than to understand them."
– Kiran Desai

The impact of words is more important than just understanding them. It is also a reminder of the emotion and beauty hidden in literature.

♡♡♡

ELEVEN

Indian Literature in Translation: An Exploration of Indian Literature in Other Languages

India, the world's most populous democracy, is home to robust literary cultures spanning multiple languages, communities and landscapes. As a result, Indian literature has a varied, complex history that reflects the many linguistic and cultural influences that have informed the nation throughout its history. The works of Indian writers have, in turn, been translated into numerous languages, allowing their stories and perspectives to spread internationally.

Since the early colonial period and the development of the English language in India, Indian literature has seen a great deal of international exposure. English-language translations of Indian authors like Rabindranath Tagore and Arundhati Roy have won accolades, especially in the West, though not to the exclusion of works in other languages. Could, Premchand, and Mulk Raj Anand have all been widely read in the West through translations into languages like French and German.

Nevertheless, other, less familiar languages and literary traditions have been largely overlooked by the Western world over the years. Much of India's literature is spoken in languages other than English, such as Hindi, Bengali, Gujarati, Kannada and Telugu, as well as minority languages like Rajasthani, Tamil and Assamese. Indian literature in these non-English languages has gradually been gaining more recognition after years of neglect.

More recently, Indian literature in translation has become known in other countries through the emergence of global Indian diasporas. Stories and poems in languages such as Tamil, Gujarati, Hindi and other Indian languages can be researched and appreciated by scholars and readers virtually anywhere in the world. In addition, social media's vast potential for dissemination also has opened up new avenues for the translation and introduction of non-

English language Indian literature on a truly international scale.

Given India's rich and varied literary traditions, it is important that the country's writers, poets and storytellers in both English and non-English languages receive the recognition they deserve. Indian literature in translation is a vital avenue for promoting the appreciation of India's literary heritage both at home and abroad, and for further enriching our cultural understanding of the society we live in. With the continued development of local, regional and global networks of translation and cultural exchange, India's literatures can increasingly be shared, celebrated, and enjoyed around the world.

"Writers must know when to stop writing."
- Ruskin Bond

Sometimes, we just need to take a break and rejuvenate ourselves in order to write effectively.

♡♡♡

TWELVE

An Overview of Indian Literature: From Ancient to Modern Times

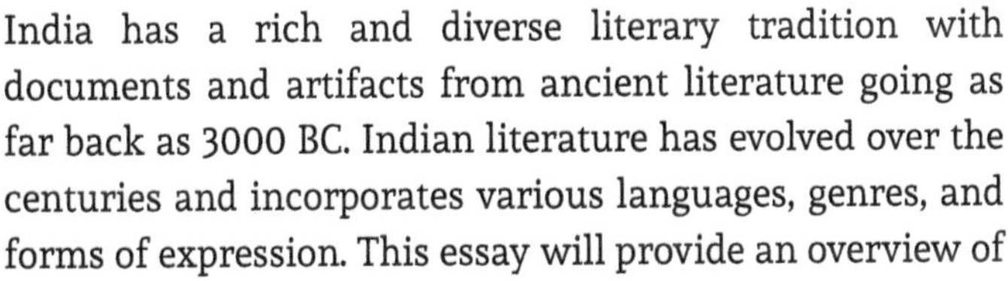

India has a rich and diverse literary tradition with documents and artifacts from ancient literature going as far back as 3000 BC. Indian literature has evolved over the centuries and incorporates various languages, genres, and forms of expression. This essay will provide an overview of Indian literature from ancient times to the present day.

Ancient Indian literature can be divided into two categories: Sanskrit epics and classical works. Sanskrit epics such as the Ramayana, the Mahabharata, and the Puranas are some of India's most revered texts and are associated with aspects of social and religious life in India. In addition, these epics provided the basis for numerous works of art such as theatre, dance, and music. Alongside the Sanskrit epics, ancient India was also home to a number of classical works written in Vedic, Apabhramsa and later in Prakrit. These works cover topics such as philosophy, medicine, astrology, and law and include the Upanishads, Kavya, Sahitya, and Smriti.

As India entered the medieval period, Persian and Arabic-influenced literature flourished due to the presence of Islamic invaders. This led to the emergence of a new genre, ghazal, which is a type of Urdu love poetry. During this time period, several prolific writers such as Mirza Ghalib, Amir Khusrau, and Mir Taqi Mir composed many works of literature. In addition, the advent of the Mughal Empire and the advent of Sufism in India saw the rise of many religious and spiritual works such as the writings of Sufi saints such as Rahim and Rumi.

India's modern literature can be divided into two distinct categories. The first is Indian English literature, which consists of novels, stories, poetry, and plays written by authors in English. Authors such as Arun Joshi, Vikram Seth, and Rohinton Mistry are some of the most prominent figures in contemporary Indian English literature. The second is Regional Indian literature, which is written in vernacular languages such as Hindi, Marathi, Bengali, and Gujarati. While Regional Indian literature has lost some of its momentum in recent times due to the emergence of Indian English literature, there are still some notable authors and works such as Mulk Raj Anand, Raja Rao and Laxmi Prasad Devkota.

To conclude, Indian literature has evolved over the centuries, incorporating various languages, genres, and forms of expression. Ancient Indian literature consisted of works such as the Sanskrit epics and classical works while the medieval period saw a flourishing of Persian and Arabic-influenced literature. Modern Indian literature can be divided into Indian English literature and Regional Indian literature, with notable authors and works in both categories. Altogether, Indian literature is an immense anthology of unique and immensely influential works.

Other Books Of The Author

1. The Moments When I Met God
2. Kashiyile Theertha Pathangal
3. GURU GYAN VANI
4. Abhiprerak Gita
5. ASSI SE JAIN GHAT TAK
6. Hopelessness of Arjuna
7. The Soul and It's True Nature
8. Sense of Action (Karma)
9. Action through Wisdom
10. Action through Wisdom
11. THEORY AND PRACTICAL OF EVERY ACTION
12. LOGICAL UNDERSTANDING OF THE SUPREME
13. THE IMPERISHABLE SUPREME
14. Yatra Nishadraj se Hanuman Ghat Tak
15. Yatra Karnatak Ghat se Raja Ghat Tak
16. Yatra Pandey Ghat se Prayagraj Ghat Tak
17. Yatra Ranjendra Prasad Ghat se Dattatreya Ghat Tak
18. YaatraSindhiya Ghat se Gwaliar Ghat Tak
19. Yatra Mangala Gauri Ghat se Hanuman Gadhi Ghat Tak
20. Yatra Gaay Ghat Se Nishad Ghat Tak
21. MAA GANGA, GHATEN EVM UTSAV
22. Ganga Arti Dev Deepavali evam Any Utsav
23. Potentials of Digitalized India
24. VEDIC CONSCIOUSNESS
25. A Brief Introduction to Vedic Science
26. Kashi ke Barah Jyotirling
27. IMPACT OF MOTIVATION
28. Let's have a Milky Way Journey
29. Color Therapy in a Nutshell

30. Rigveda in a Nutshell
31. Yajurveda in a Nutshell
32. Samveda in a Nutshell
33. Atharva Veda in a Nutshell
34. Ayushman Bhava - Ayurveda
35. Srimad Bhagavad Gita and Upanishad Connection
36. Srimad Bhagavad Gita - an attempt to summarize each chapter.
37. Facts and Impact of Nakshatra
38. Astro Gems - NAVARATNA
39. Ekadashi - A Concise Overview
40. A Concise View of Hanuman Chalisa
41. Inspirational Gita
42. Nakshatraranyam
43. Summary of 18 Mahapuranas
44. Synopsis of 18 Upa Puranas
45. Rigvediya Upanishads
46. Shukla Yajurvediya Upanishads
47. Krishna Yajurvediya Upanishads
48. Samavediya Upanishads
49. Atharvavediya Upanishads
50. The Seven Great Sages
51. From Rocket Scientist to President Dr. APJ Abdul Kalam
52. The Visionary's Voice - Quotes of Dr. APJ Abdul Kalam
53. The Wisdom of Swami Vivekananda: Insights and Inspiration from a Legendary Spiritual Teacher
54. Ayurvedic Remedies from the Garden
55. Sages and Seers
56. Rising Strong – Motivational Stories of Women
57. Beyond Flames -Mystery stories of Funeral Ghat Manikarnika
58. The Origins of Tulsi: A Look at the Mythological Roots of the Plant"

59. The Holistic Cow: A Look at the Physical, Spiritual, and Cultural Importance of Cows in India
60. Arts of Healing
61. Exploring the Divine
62. Understanding Five Elements
63. The Etymology of Ram
64. Symbols of India
65. Voice of Change (About Speeches of Great Men)
66. She Speaks (About Speeches of Great Women)
67. **Patriotism on Celluloid – Brief About Patriotic Films**
68. **The Music of Motivation: A Brief Guide to Inspirational Film Songs**
69. **Unlocking the Secrets of the Dashopanishads**
70. A Cultural Mosaic
71. Ancient Traditions, Modern Minds
72. Ecos of Ancient Wisdom
73. Beneath the Surface
74. From Temples to Ashrams
75. Sages of the Subcontinent
76. The Art of Healling (Ayurveda, Yoga & Naturopathy)
77. Indian Kitchen
78. The Festivals of India
79. The Indian Epics Retold
80. The Power of Mantras
81. The Indian River Ganges
82. The Indian Architecture
83. Rites of Passage
84. The Indian Silk Road
85. The Indian Literature
86. The Indian Villages
87. The Indian Folks & Crafts

Contact

DR. JAGADEESH PILLAI

PhD in Vedic Science

Four Times Guinness World Record Holder

Winner of Mahatma Gandhi Vishwa Shanti Puraskar and Global Peace Ambassador

Gemology, Astro & Vastu Consultant - Spiritual Counselor

Consultant for designing World Record Ideas

Efficient Tarot Card Reader

9839093003

myrichindia@gmail.com

drjagadeeshpillai@facebook

drjagadeeshpillai@instagram

jagadeeshpillai@youtube

www. JAGADEESHPILLAI.com

|| LOKAHA SAMASTHAHA SUKHINO BHAVANTU ||

www.ingramcontent.com/pod-product-compliance
Ingram Content Group UK Ltd.
Pitfield, Milton Keynes, MK11 3LW, UK
UKHW041844200726
13854UKWH00005BA/2058